Little Mitchie

WHY DO CATS MEOW?

DO YOU EVER WONDER ABOUT ANIMALS?

KIM THOMPSON

CREATING YOUNG NONFICTION READERS

Little Mitchie books spark curiosity and support early nonfiction reading for students in Grades 2-3. Designed to build vocabulary, support second language learners, and prepare readers for middle-grade content, each book includes helpful tips for parents and educators to build confidence and deepen understanding of the world.

TIPS FOR READING NONFICTION WITH BEGINNING READERS

Talk about Nonfiction

Begin by explaining that nonfiction books give us information that is true. The book will be organized around a specific topic or idea, and we may learn new facts through reading.

Look at the Parts

Most nonfiction books have helpful features. Our *Little Mitchie* titles include color photographs and graphic aids, a table of contents, a glossary, and an index. Share the purpose of these features with your reader.

Color Photos and Graphic Aids

A lot of information can be found by "reading" photos, charts, maps, and other graphic aids found within nonfiction texts. Help your reader learn more about the different ways information can be displayed.

Table of Contents

Located at the front of the book, this list shows the big ideas within the text and the page numbers where they can be found.

Glossary

Located at the back of the book, the glossary defines key words and phrases that are related to the topic. These words and phrases can be found in the text in colored type.

Index

Located at the back of the book, an index is an alphabetical list of topics and the page numbers where they can be found.

With a little help and guidance about reading nonfiction, you can feel good about introducing a young reader to the world of *Little Mitchie* nonfiction books.

Little Mitchie is an imprint of:

Mitchell Lane PUBLISHERS

2001 SW 31st Avenue
Hallandale, FL 33009
mitchelllanepub.com

First Edition, 2027.

Author: Kim Thompson
Designer: Jen Bowers

Library of Congress Cataloging-in-Publication Data
Title: Why Do Cats Meow? / by Kim Thompson

Description: Hallandale, FL :
Mitchell Lane Publishers, [2027]

Identifiers:
ISBN 979-8-89260-924-1 (library bound)
ISBN 979-8-89260-979-1 (eBook)

Library of Congress Control Number: 2026936380

PHOTO CREDITS
Shutterstock: cover, p.1 ©2020 Viktoria77777, p.5 ©2016 Marko Radenkovic, p.6–7, 22 ©2025 Padodo, p.9 ©2010 Sue McDonald, p.10–11 ©2021 OlgaBartashevich, p.13 ©2014 Ermolaev Alexander, p.14, 22 ©2018 Anna Krivitskaya, p.17, 22 ©2020 Natalya Biryukova, p.18 ©2007 Eric Isselee, p.19 ©2019 New Africa, p.21 ©2014 Alena Ozerova, p.22 ©2024 Nynke van Holten

TABLE OF CONTENTS

Chapter One

QUESTIONS

Have you ever spent time with a pet cat? Did you wish it could talk to you?

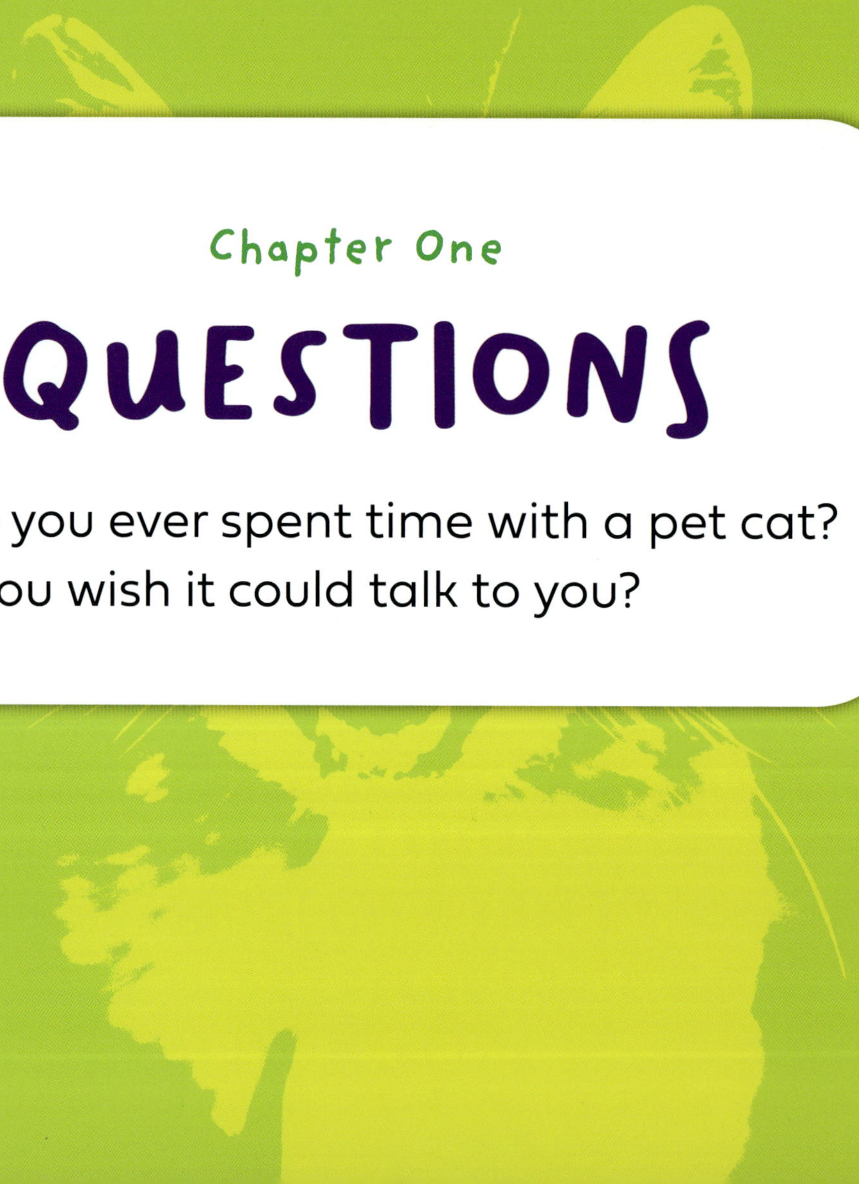

You probably wondered about cat **communication**. You may have asked these questions.

1. What do cats have to say?
2. Why do cats meow?
3. Do cats use **body language**?

Chapter Two

MOMMY, HELP!

Like all animals, cats have feelings. They have wants and needs. Cats communicate to say things like, “Help me” or “I want a treat!”

Tiny kittens use **vocalizations** with their mothers. A mother calls to her kittens with **chirping** or trilling sounds. When a kitten wants something from its mother, it meows.

ANIMAL WONDER

Kittens are born with their eyes closed. Sound is an important way for them to interact with the world.

Chapter Three

MEOW OR YOWL?

Most adult cats do not meow to each other. They only meow to people.

Cats remember being kittens. They remember that meowing is a way to get what they want. Now, they meow to you. They see you as a big cat mother!

ANIMAL WONDER

To **purr**, a cat vibrates muscles in the throat and chest while breathing in and out. Cats purr when they are **content**. They purr to comfort themselves when they are in pain.

ANIMAL WONDER

After birds, cats are some of the noisiest animals. They use over 100 different vocalizations.

Cats make many sounds. When they see a bird, they chatter with excitement. When they are in trouble, they yowl. If they growl or **hiss**, stand back! They feel **threatened**. They may swipe or bite.

Chapter Four

WATCH AND LEARN

A cat also uses **visual** communication. Watch the cat's ears. They turn toward whatever the cat is noticing. They twitch when a cat is **nervous**. They flatten and point backward when a cat is afraid.

A cat's tail says a lot. Happy cats hold their tails straight up. Excited cats swish their tails from side to side. When a cat is afraid, its tail puffs up.

ANIMAL WONDER

How do you know if a cat really trusts you? It will lie on its back and show you its belly.

Chapter Five

ANSWERS

Now, you can answer your questions.

1. **WHAT DO CATS HAVE TO SAY?**

   Cats communicate to show their feelings and ask for what they need and want.

2. **WHY DO CATS MEOW?**

   A cat meows to tell a person what it wants.

3. **DO CATS USE BODY LANGUAGE?**

   Yes. Cats move their bodies in different ways to show their feelings.

ANIMAL WONDER

Keep asking questions about animals. That's how you learn about the amazing creatures that share our world!

CAT COMMUNICATION CHART

BODY LANGUAGE

RELAXED

CAUTIOUS

FRIGHTENED

THREATENED

VOCALIZATIONS

Chatter: I am excited.
Chirp or trill: Come here.
Hiss or growl: Stay away!

Meow: I need my person.
Purr: I am content.
Yowl: I am in trouble.

GLOSSARY

body language (BAH-dee LANG-gwij) body movements used to show feelings and communicate with others

chirping (CHUR-ping) making a high-pitched sound like a bird

communication (kuh-myoo-ni-KAY-shuhn) sharing thoughts, feelings, and information with others

content (kuhn-TENT) peaceful and happy; satisfied

hiss (his) to make a long *sss* sound like a snake, especially to show unhappiness

nervous (NUR-vuhs) worried, scared, or anxious

purr (pur) to make a continuous, low, vibrating sound

threatened (THRET-uhnd) feeling scared or in danger

visual (VIZH-oo-uhl) related to seeing; able to be seen

vocalizations (voh-kuh-li-ZAY-shuhnz) sounds that have meaning

FURTHER READING

Mattice, Lindy. *How to Speak Animal: Decode the Secret Language of Dogs, Cats, Birds, Reptiles, and More!* Bushel and Peck Books, 2022.

Newman, Aline Alexander. *How to Speak Cat: A Guide to Decoding Cat Language.* National Geographic Kids, 2015.

ON THE INTERNET

BBC Earth Kids: Are These Cats Actually Speaking?
youtube.com/watch?v=17f_81LcnKM
Watch cats as they try to communicate with people.

Pet Place: Just for Kids: How Your Cat Communicates
petplace.com/article/cats/just-for-fun/just-for-kids-how-your-cat-communicates
A complete guide to understanding your cat.

That's So Montessori: 33 Cat Facts for Kids
thatssomontessori.com/cat-facts-for-kids
Learn fascinating cat facts.

INDEX